The practical curriculum

SCHOOLS COUNCIL WORKING PAPER 70

The practical curriculum

a report from the Schools Council

Methuen Educational

First published 1981 for the Schools Council
160 Great Portland Street, London W1N 6LL
by Methuen Educational
11 New Fetter Lane, London EC4P 4EE

Filmset by
Northumberland Press Ltd
Gateshead, Tyne and Wear
Printed in Great Britain by
Richard Clay (The Chaucer Press) Ltd
Bungay, Suffolk

British Library Cataloguing in Publication Data

Schools Council
The practical curriculum. – (Schools Council
Working papers; 70 ISSN 0533–1668)
1. Curriculum planning – England
375.00942   LB1570
ISBN 0–423–50900–4

Contents

Foreword

When the Council decided its programme priorities in 1979, having consulted the local authorities, teachers and its other member interests, it considered that 'there appears to be support for developing a general framework for the curriculum. We propose to engage in discussions about curriculum balance and content. We believe that teachers, schools and local education authorities will welcome a lead from the Council.'

We hope that this document will provide that stimulating lead, and will result in local discussion of the fundamental issues in curriculum planning for pupils of all ages and conditions.

The report contains the reflections of a working party whose members represented a wide cross-section of Council committees. Their comments and conclusions were made as individuals with deep knowledge and experience of the education system, rather than as representatives of organizations or institutions.

The working party, from the outset, decided to address the broadest possible readership, and particularly teachers with a responsibility for and interest in designing the curriculum.

We also decided that the text should be as short and as readable as possible, since the intention is to encourage people to take in an overall view of what is a complex activity before deciding where to sharpen their focus. We hope we may have found a way of presenting the curriculum as an activity and not merely a syllabus or an exhortation.

Our report is not intended to be either definitive or prescriptive; indeed, we hope it will provoke discussion and provide new insights especially in an area where it is accepted that there is more than one solution. We shall be delighted to have comments which would enable us to prepare a second edition embodying additional useful material.

This document was not easy to conceive, or to write. I wish to thank the members of the working party who gave unstintingly of time and effort; and we all wish to record our gratitude to the Council staff for their labours and inspiration in drafting and re-drafting.

JOHN TOMLINSON
Chairman, Schools Council

Introduction

The background to this paper is the vigorous curriculum debate of recent years. In 1976 a speech by the Prime Minister, James Callaghan, at Ruskin College, Oxford, marked the beginning of the Great Debate. As a nation we discussed a whole curriculum, a common curriculum, a core and a framework. We read about dilemmas of the curriculum, controlling the curriculum and regenerating the curriculum. In 1979 Her Majesty's Inspectors described their own *View of the Curriculum*, in which they presented the essence of their surveys of primary and secondary schools.

The discussion was taken a stage further in 1980 when the Government published a consultative paper, *A Framework for the School Curriculum*. Though the Government believe that the variations between what is taught in different schools are too great, they emphasized that they did 'not intend to alter the existing statutory relationship between the various partners'. They hoped their consultative paper would help in reaching a national consensus about the curriculum. Following discussions with teachers' organizations, local authority associations, representatives of industry and the Schools Council, the Government was preparing to issue a second statement of their views as our own paper went to press early in 1981.

The Schools Council has a distinctive contribution to make to this discussion. It is the only national forum where representatives of central government, local authorities, teachers' organizations, further education and higher education, employers, trade unions, parents, churches and examining bodies meet to discuss the content and process of education in school. This blend of knowledge and experience equips the Council to make a unique contribution to discussion about the curriculum.

The Council believes there is a need for a visible structure for the curriculum. A useful starting point is to consider each pupil's right of access to different areas of human knowledge and experience. The heart of the matter is what each child takes away from school. For each of them, what he or she takes away is the effective curriculum. This paper

9

therefore emphasizes this different view of the curriculum as the experience each child has at school and what each takes away.

Our paper consists of four chapters and a conclusion. The first chapter explains why we believe a structure is needed and why we think subjects are a sensible way of interpreting curricular aims and policies. There are other ways of thinking about the curriculum, and we go on to discuss the contribution some of these can make to a rationale for the curriculum. Teachers need to know the principles which underpin their school's curriculum, and to be clear about what they hope and plan their pupils will achieve. Introducing their pupils to different kinds of experience and different forms of knowledge, making use of different modes of teaching and learning, developing values and attitudes, and teaching skills, including many non-verbal skills, are among the possible ways of approaching a curriculum. We believe schools should try to look at their curriculum from each of these positions. We are concerned above all with the view each pupil has of the curriculum he or she experiences, and what parts of that experience the pupil takes away.

Chapter II is about planning a curriculum. Chapter III suggests several ways of monitoring this curriculum and Chapter IV is about assessing a school's success.

We have tried to say a great deal in a short paper, and have not repeated points even though they may be relevant at several stages of the discussion.

We have come increasingly to see this as the first of a series in which different papers might deal in greater detail with particular issues. Even in writing this paper we felt how hard it is to say anything about curriculum or organization which applies equally to nursery, primary and secondary schools. We are therefore planning to follow this introductory paper with others on particular stages of schooling and different aspects of the curriculum.

In the conclusion we invite comments on this and other suggestions for further work by the Council. We shall be delighted to have comments particularly if they enable us to prepare a second edition of this paper, and other papers, embodying additional useful material.

Many people play a part in shaping what happens in schools. They include parents, governors, employers and others in the local community, education committees and their advisers and officers. We hope they will find helpful these suggestions for deciding and monitoring the curriculum.

This contribution to the curriculum debate is addressed first of all, however, to teachers. Teachers are at the sharp end of education. They are the people who have to resolve the tensions between the delivery of a mass public service open to all children, and the individuality of each child. The relation between teachers and children is at the heart of education in schools. Whatever the outcome of the discussion on freedom and uniformity in the curriculum, many important decisions about what is taught and how it is taught will still be made by schools, and by individual teachers. They cannot avoid, and most are anxious to claim, responsibility for deciding how to teach. They need a good basis for these decisions. That is what we have tried to provide here.

This is therefore a handbook of working papers to help teachers to test their own ideas and develop them. It is an incitement to critical self-evaluation, a way for schools to develop their capacity to respond to changes in their environment. We thought the paper would be more useful if we made clear what our own views are. In doing this we have tried to make a whetstone for teachers to use, not a prescription to take.

I.   A rationale for the curriculum

A realistic discussion of what is taught in schools needs to start from where we are, not where we might or ought to be. Schools for young children usually organize their work through class teachers: older pupils tend to organize theirs through subject departments. Subjects are therefore a natural entry to the curriculum of a secondary school. In practice many teachers of young children also seem to find it helpful to think about their work in terms of subjects.

   This thinking will surely be more productive if teachers have a clear idea of what they are trying to achieve and how they will know whether they have been successful. We recognize the hazards in recommending a purely rational process of planning and review. In ordinary human affairs people rarely start with clear aims or a clear view of how they will know whether they have been successful. They are more likely to start thinking about these things in the light of their everyday experience. Experience and thought can reinforce each other in a systematic process of clarifying aims, refining methods and assessing success.

Underlying principles

We believe there are powerful arguments for trying to agree what principles the curriculum should rest on. In whatever part of the country they live, and whether they are girls or boys, children have the same rights, and should enjoy much the same opportunities for education. If children share similar experiences and knowledge, we believe there will be greater cohesion between different social groups and between the generations. And it will certainly be convenient for some parents if there is more in common between schools wherever they are. Most important of the practical arguments for agreeing underlying principles, and basing action on them, is that this may be the only way of guaranteeing an effective curriculum for every child.

13

The Council recognizes *six central issues in working out a curriculum:*

i the overwhelming need, for each school and for the country as a whole, is to find a rationale for the curriculum now every child has a right to eleven years' education;

ii then to identify the irreducible minimum to which every pupil should have a right of access; the Council believes this minimum should reflect the complex diversity of human nature and the capacity schools have to contribute to every aspect of personal and social growth. The minimum curriculum should be broad and stimulating;

iii to decide what mix of subject disciplines and *kinds of experience* a school should provide to meet the diverse needs of its pupils, and to achieve a reasonable balance over the eleven years of compulsory schooling;

iv to take account of the implications of having externally examined outcomes for most pupils;

v to negotiate a match between the desired curriculum and the staff, accommodation, equipment and materials available; and

vi to think out ways of discovering whether the planned curriculum achieves what is hoped of it.

We have referred deliberately to schools instead of education. There are other paths to knowledge and education than school. The influences of home, neighbourhood, peers and the media ofter greatly exceed the influence of school. Children spend a relatively small part of their lives at school, and most leave school before they reach maturity. These factors limit what schools can realistically hope to achieve on their own. At the same time schools have potential allies who can add greatly to their capacity for education.

Aims

There is no better general statement of the aims of education than that of the Warnock Report: 'first, to enlarge a child's knowledge, experience and imaginative understanding, and thus his awareness of moral values and capacity for enjoyment; and secondly, to enable him to enter the world after formal education is over as an active participant in society and a responsible contributor to it, capable of achieving as much independence as possible'.[1]

These aims are the same for all children: but their starting points are diverse, their speed and direction vary, and their destinations are even more diverse. Schools have to find ways of responding to this diversity, and ways of reflecting the complex make-up of individuals and society. Their aims will be correspondingly complex. *Schools have the capacity and the will to help their pupils in at least six ways:*

i to acquire knowledge, skills and practical abilities, and the will to use them;

ii to develop qualities of mind, body, spirit, feeling and imagination;

iii to appreciate human achievements in art, music, science, technology and literature;

iv to acquire understanding of the social, economic and political order, and a reasoned set of attitudes, values and beliefs;

v to prepare for their adult lives at home, at work, at leisure, and at large, as consumers and citizens;

and, most important of all:

vi to develop a sense of self-respect, the capacity to live as independent, self-motivated adults and the ability to function as contributing members of co-operative groups.

Each pupil should be moving forward, according to age and ability, in all these ways.

More specific aims are needed for each school, each year and each class. A primary school, for example, might wish each of its pupils to learn:

i to read fluently and accurately, with understanding, feeling and discrimination;

ii to develop a legible style of handwriting and satisfactory standards of spelling, syntax, punctuation and usage;

iii to communicate clearly and confidently in speech and writing, in ways appropriate for various occasions and purposes;

iv to listen attentively and with understanding;

v to learn how to acquire information from various sources, and to record information and findings in various ways;

vi to apply computational skills with speed and accuracy;

vii to understand the applications of mathematical ideas in various situations in home, classroom, school and local area;

viii to observe living and inanimate things, and to recognize characteristics such as pattern and order;

ix to master basic scientific ideas;

x to investigate solutions and interpret evidence, to analyse and to solve problems;

xi to develop awareness of self and sensitivity to others, acquire a set of

moral values and the confidence to make and hold to moral judgements, and develop habits of self-discipline and acceptable behaviour;

xii to be aware of the geographical, historical and social aspects of the
local environment and the national heritage, and to be aware of other
times and places;

xiii to acquire sufficient control of self or of tools, equipment and
instruments to be able to use music, drama and several forms of arts
and crafts as means of expression;

xiv to develop agility and physical co-ordination, confidence in and
through physical activity, and the ability to express feeling through
movement.

This is necessarily a short and rather general set of aims. Schools may
be able to extend or vary it to meet their own needs.

We would commend particularly the following version of curriculum
aims suggested for some young people of 16 and 17. With modification
some of these aims would be appropriate for pupils of other ages. The
teaching and learning process should lead each of them towards:

i levels of achievement in literacy and numeracy to meet the basic
demands of contemporary society;

ii an appropriate development of physical and manipulative skills in
both vocational and leisure contexts, and an appreciation of those
skills in others;

iii an ability to be sensitive to the needs of others in order to develop
satisfactory personal relationships;

iv a capacity to approach various kinds of problems methodically and
effectively, to undertake courses of action, evaluate them and modify
those actions accordingly;

v a reasoned set of social and moral values applicable to issues in
contemporary society;

vi the capacity to make informed, responsible and realistic decisions
with respect to his or her immediate future;

vii sufficient political and economic literacy to understand the social
environment and contribute to its development, and to be aware of
international issues;

viii competence in a variety of learning skills;

ix recognition of his or her physical and technological environments,
the relationship between these and the needs of mankind in general
and working life in particular, leading to his or her capacity to use
and modify these environments;

x the necessary skills for coping with everyday problems together with the ability to collaborate with others and to contribute to their well-being;

xi an informed perspective of the role and status of a young person in adult society and the world of work and as a member of communities;

xii a flexibility of attitudes and ability to learn sufficient to cope with future changes in technology and careers.[2]

Teachers are likely to have aims like these for each class they teach, and each pupil in those classes. Teachers of young children usually take a whole class for a year. This means they are well placed to have an overview of each child's progress towards these aims, and how each activity contributes to progress towards each aim. The way most secondary schools organize their work makes it harder for them to take this kind of synoptic view of what the curriculum is for each child. One step towards linking the school's overall aims and the experience of each child would be for the teachers of each year group to agree an explicit statement of aims for the year group. The teachers of each class might agree a similar statement for the class.

Statements like these and a general statement of aims for each school would provide a basis for self-assessment and for discussing the need for resources. A statement of curricular aims is the best basis for teachers, governors and their local authority to discuss and agree the provision of staff, accommodation, equipment, materials and cash.

Learning through experience

In addition to thinking about aims, teachers also have to think about planning and organizing their pupils' learning. How they do this seems to depend on their pupils' age.

Teachers of young children usually plan a varied programme of activities for their pupils. Each activity represents a different way in which children can experience and get to know the world around them. One of the Schools Council's projects, Science 5–13, has shown in *Early Experiences* how appropriate activities can help to foster scientific ideas in children of 5 or 6.

Firstly, embedded in the activities themselves are things that are basically scientific. Children building an Indian totem pole from boxes, for example, must consider the size of the boxes and which surfaces will fit best for stability. Even a simple wall built from blocks must be vertical for stability, and certain arrangements of blocks are more stable than others.

Which wall is easiest to knock over?

Who can make the tallest tower of bricks?

Secondly, science is the handmaiden that helps in an activity. For example, having made a model lighthouse it is fun to set a light flashing from it.[3]

Work with water provides experience of some of its physical properties, such as transparency and fluidity, opportunities of measuring different volumes of water and understanding how volume is conserved, opportunities of testing which things float and sink in water, and what effect water has on other things.

The experience of trying to make castles, pies or heaps with wet and dry sand, weighing it, measuring its mass and its volume, and comparing sand with other soils, all offer starting points for acquiring scientific knowledge and insight into scientific concepts.

Cooking provides experience of liquids and solids, wet and dry things, hot and cold things, smelling and tasting, mixing solids and liquids, weighing and timing. From all these, and from other activities like measuring, making and growing things, looking at and looking after things, children of 6 and 7 begin to acquire scientific experience.

Early explorations of their environment teach children to look around them, to touch and to feel, to listen, smell and taste. They learn to make and arrange collections: of wild flowers, grasses, twigs, leaves, seeds, fruits, animal tracks, stones, fossils, soils and countless other things. They learn to classify and sort their collections. They might divide the things that fall from trees into scales, petals, seeds and leaves, and classify the leaves by colour, size or shape. A knowledge of sets and subsets comes early when learned like this.[4]

The main concern of infant teachers is to help their pupils to explore their immediate environment and find the words to describe and discuss it effectively. 'Children learn what becomes available to them through their experiences,' wrote Joan Tough in *Talking and Learning*. Only the teacher's professional skill can ensure that experience leads to scientific understanding and skill in communicating. 'What is said to children as they are watching and imitating, the explanations given, the information supplied and the encouragement to think in certain ways will affect whatever learning the child is accomplishing and will have implications for his future learning. The child's experiences of using language with others may extend or curtail his ability to make sense of what he experiences. The child's thinking skills may be extended, or they may be restricted, by what is said to him.'[5]

The success of a nursery or infant school is rightly measured by how its teachers help their pupils to a wide and active experience of their world, and what their pupils learn from this experience.

Her Majesty's Inspectors' survey of primary schools[6] showed how important this is for older pupils too. The schools whose children did best at the basics were those which emphasized other kinds of experience too, in art, music, history, geography and science. In educational development, the privileged are those whose experience stimulates their imagination, extends their use of language, demands thought and illustrates new concepts.

There is of course a close link between these different kinds of experience of the world and many familiar school subjects. Unfortunately teachers of older children have often tended to emphasize the content of their subjects instead of their importance as ways of experiencing and knowing the real world.

Forms of knowledge

Reacting against this kind of approach, some writers have suggested basing the curriculum on different forms of knowledge rather than subjects. They often identify several such forms of knowledge and go on to argue that every pupil ought to experience each of the identified areas.

One such attempt identified seven areas of knowledge: human studies; philosophy; moral judgement and awareness; religious understanding; formal logic and mathematics; physical sciences; and aesthetic experience.[7] Another, more immediately related to a curriculum for schools, identified five main areas: humanities and social science; moral education; mathematics; physical and biological sciences; and expressive and creative arts.[8]

In a similar analysis, in their book *Curriculum 11–16* Her Majesty's Inspectors identified eight 'areas of experience'. These were: spiritual; ethical; physical; aesthetic and creative; mathematical; linguistic; social; and political.[9]

Teachers may find it helpful to consider first whether the curriculum in their own school does include all these forms of knowledge or areas of experience and whether every pupil has opportunities of learning something of each.

Another way of building on these attempts to classify knowledge and experience is to see whether they fall short in any way of what a school would like to achieve. Some may feel, for example, that the historical, geographical and economic differ so greatly that every pupil ought to have a chance of tasting each of them. A school might wish to emphasize also the intuitive and imaginative, or the practical and technological. We believe schools ought to have all these in mind and include them in their pupils' educational experience.

In particular we would suggest that every boy and girl should sample the three distinct elements of craft, design and technology. We emphasize these because we believe that working with materials and designing and making solutions to problems are distinct kinds of experience and learning. It is important for schools to cultivate these kinds of learning as well as their pupils' ability to experience and interpret reality with all five senses. For some pupils ear, eye and touch are as important ways of gaining experience as reading is for others. Whatever their abilities, pupils can learn some things only through concrete and practical experience.

We therefore believe schools ought to help all their pupils to experience as many as possible of the forms of knowledge mentioned in this section. It will not be possible to maintain them all for eleven years. But it should be possible at least to introduce them all at some stage, and to unveil something of the scope for creative activity in every kind of activity.

Modes of teaching and learning

Teachers find it as hard to know how to teach effectively as to know what to teach. The heart of the problem is how to match language, content, method and process to the pupils' differing ages and stages of development. Each teacher has to try to cater for differences in levels of attainment, speed of learning and emergent interests. Nor do pupils necessarily reach the various states of development in the same order or at the same speed.

To meet these challenges a teacher needs to be able to call on an extensive repertoire of teaching and learning methods. Crude descriptions of teaching as progressive or traditional, exploratory or didactic fail to convey the variety and range of modes of teaching and learning teachers have at their command. Some pupils may respond well to one mode, and others to different modes. They and their teachers are more likely to enjoy school, and stay on their toes, if their days and weeks are varied by skilful choice of mode. Sometimes the mode or process of learning has its own lessons, more potent than the formal subject-matter of the lesson.

Children may work individually or in groups, their contribution may be active or receptive, their work practical, experiential or theoretical, located in or out of the classroom. Young children learn much from play and interaction with their peers, role play, making and doing, storytelling and learning by rote. These remain important as other modes are introduced. These modes include direct instruction by lecture or dictated notes and the use of resources like books, documents, audio-visual material, laboratory or workshop material, the natural and man-made environment for work ranging from short exercises to substantial projects, sometimes directed, sometimes independent, sometimes co-operative. As pupils grow older rational thought and analysis, criticism and evaluation, quantitative analysis, testing hypotheses, problem-solving, modelling and simulation become increasingly important.

Some aspects of social and moral education arise from a school's organization, structure and reward system, its ethos, the example its older members set, and the interaction of pupil with teacher, pupil with pupil and school with community.

Some of the attitudes, skills and understanding society values most, such as respect for others' opinions, the ability to communicate and relate successfully to other people, practical capability and the ability to solve problems, arise from the process rather than the content of education. This needs to be recognized. Understanding these processes and practising them successfully in a well-planned and balanced curriculum requires sustained thought and application. These are expert and professional matters.

Values and attitudes

Schools have a great capacity for social, personal and moral education. But they should neither seek, nor be charged with, total responsibility. In these areas above all the influence of home, neighbourhood and contemporary society is strong. In these areas, too, the pluralism of contemporary society may be reflected in differing views among the teachers in a school.

Despite these differences schools need to focus on personal and social development because maturity is a prerequisite for acquiring, interpreting and practising knowledge, skill and experience.

Each school ought to decide what values and attitudes it wishes to emphasize. These are matters which teachers should discuss with their pupils' parents and the local community. In doing so teachers may find it helpful to compare their own thoughts with certain qualities we believe are important:

  i sensitivity to language and the arts, to the environment and to other people;
  ii sympathy with and insight into other cultures and peoples;
  iii altruism, or the capacity to put other people's interests before one's own;
  iv curiosity and enthusiasm;
  v responsibility or self-discipline;

vi independence in making moral judgements;
vii the capacity to come to a reasoned judgement;
viii intolerance of cruelty and cant.

Agreeing what values and attitudes a school would like to promote may be relatively easy. Thinking out how to promote them through all its varied programmes and activities is among the most important and the hardest tasks a school faces. If a school is to be successful in this aspect of its work above all it needs a consistent, across-the-board approach to which all normal programmes and subjects contribute.

Schools sometimes pursue aims such as these through programmes of health, moral or social education. Very often teachers take a conscious decision to develop health or moral or social education across the curriculum, through the teaching of several subjects. This is a good approach to these difficult aspects of education, but it cannot succeed without the appropriate subject teachers being ready to review the content of their teaching. Even that is not sufficient. Some values, like those of democracy, tolerance and responsibility, grow only with experience of them. Social education arises from a school's ethos, its organization and its relation with its community. The way a school organizes its staff and pupils, and its formal rules, say a great deal about its real values and attitudes. Schools need to practise what they seek to promote.

Skills

A skill is more than knowing, and more than knowing how. It is action too. A skill involves the application of knowledge to achieve some anticipated outcome. It needs the capacity and the will to act, as well as knowledge. Skill without knowledge is inconceivable, but knowledge without skill has a long, sad history. We believe schools need to make a conscious effort to ensure that their pupils acquire skills, many of which may prove to have a life-long value.

A handful of fundamental skills form the highway to education. They include initial reading and number skills, the ability to work alone and the ability to work in groups. In addition to these cognitive and personal skills members of any society need many other abilities. In our society, for example, a knowledge of political processes, the ability to interpret scientific data and the ability to make judgements on environmental issues are among the prerequisites of effective citizenship. But these abilities are not as overwhelmingly important as the first group. Unfortunately there has not been any consistent attempt to define the levels of fundamental skill, particularly in literacy and numeracy, that are needed for children to enter fully into the various stages of the normal curriculum.

In specifying the type and level of skill they intend their pupils to acquire teachers come near to setting themselves precise aims. Schools need to decide and state exactly what skills they do hope to develop in each of the main areas of experience they are concerned with. They could use statements of this kind as a basis for self-assessment. For example, in teaching language and communication a primary teacher is likely to envisage objectives for each pupil and for the whole class, in speaking, listening, writing, reading, spelling and use of normal grammar and syntax.

Looking at the curriculum in this way, as a number of skills to be mastered, provides a basis for planning as well as self-assessment. A general example may suggest how this might work in practice. One group of skills is concerned with observing, measuring, weighing, recording, interpreting and commenting. Other groups include describing and explaining, abstracting and analysing, designing, making and testing. Almost all subjects could help to develop these as well as the fundamental skills we mentioned above. In primary schools an elementary study of plants, or of children's heights and weights, could make use of all the skills mentioned here.

We believe schools ought to emphasize the development of skill. Teachers could help themselves to be more effective if they saw the pursuit of certain types and levels of skills as one of the dimensions of their curricular planning. Nothing could do more than this to ensure that the efforts of different subject specialists contributed to the same ends.

Mode of expression: verbal and non-verbal

The practical value of verbal skills is widely appreciated and hardly needs description here. The other values of verbal skills, as vehicles for thought, feeling and imagination, seem by contrast to be neglected. *Teachers ought perhaps to specify the range of verbal skills they hope to develop, as a checklist for ensuring that what they teach and how they teach are helping to develop the whole range of skills.*

Schools can also help to develop many important non-verbal skills. These too are important vehicles for thought, feeling and imagination. People often communicate by manner, gesture and inflexion, and schools can help their pupils to recognize and respond to these languages.

More important is the increasing use of images and symbols, sometimes aural, sometimes visual, in mass communication and persuasion. As part of their preparation for adult life, pupils need help in understanding this use of image and symbol, and help in developing a capacity for critical appreciation of changing fashions and of the man-made environment.

Schools can also help their pupils to express themselves in play and movement. These abilities provide opportunities for relaxation and self-expression in youth and adult life. Schools can do much to prepare their pupils for adult life by ensuring that they develop the capacity to express themselves in these non-verbal ways.

Conclusion

In this chapter we have discussed several ways of looking at the curriculum, through the underlying principles on which it rests, its aims, the kinds of experience and forms of knowledge it opens up, the modes of teaching and learning it uses, the values and attitudes it promotes, the skills and capacity for self-expression it seeks to develop. These ways of looking at the curriculum provide a basis for planning and monitoring the curriculum, and terms of reference for assessing it.

The curriculum ought to be broad if it is to serve as any sort of intro-duction to our civilization's range of knowledge. But it must be broader still in aim and concept.

Schools should certainly help their pupils to know and remember, and to feel, to be capable, to understand and to value. Schools already shoulder this broad commitment, as many of their programmes show. Preparation for adult life requires a curriculum which includes moral education as well as political and economic understanding. Human nature and contem-porary society require a curriculum which nurtures aural and visual as well as verbal skills.

The challenge we face is therefore to blend aims and process in an effective, broad and largely common curriculum. In the next chapter we turn to ways of planning this.

Checkpoints for action

1. Are the six points on p. 15 an adequate description of what a school can do to help its pupils?
2. Have the appropriate teachers worked out more detailed statements of aims for each group of pupils?
3. Which kinds of experience does the school intend to provide?
4. What mix of modes of teaching and learning does the school intend to use?
5. What values and attitudes is the school trying to develop?

6. To what extent have teachers been able to specify skills for each area and level of the curriculum?
7. What is the extent of the school's commitment to developing non-verbal modes of expression?
8. Has the school developed or adopted a coherent written rationale for its curriculum?

II. Planning the curriculum

This chapter is about how a school might set about planning its curriculum. We consider seven kinds of problem in planning. The most demanding is to match the curriculum to each child's development. Equally difficult, in a different way, is to identify and come to terms with certain obstacles to achieving the aims a school has agreed on; this may require negotiation or even some modification of the original aims. Organizing the planning, learning to talk about the curriculum, winning commitment and finding resources are more straightforward. A note on planning in action describes how four schools have tackled some of these problems. Then we turn to the last step in planning a curriculum, translating aims and hopes into a working timetable, often the most visible statement of a school's curricular thinking.

We end the chapter with a note about where to find help.

Problem one: matching curriculum and child achievement

In describing their curricula to parents, governors and the local community, schools usually like to emphasize the range and choice of subjects offered. For the pupils, what the school provides within that range for each pupil is more important. The challenge is for a school's staff to find ways of planning each child's curriculum as a whole, and for someone on the staff to know and to monitor what happens.

The curriculum needs to fit the child. As John Brierley says: 'There is great variation in the way a normal child develops both physically, mentally and emotionally but the same milestones are passed more slowly in some children, faster in others.'[1] By the time they first go to school children have developed reasoning powers, memory and the ability to learn from experience, and a range of physical and manipulative skills. As they grow, and particularly when they reach puberty, each child changes greatly in size, physiology and social behaviour. The children in a typical class of

12-year-olds vary greatly in size, strength, shape, sexual maturity and behaviour. Some may find it hard to cope with these differences, and may even regard themselves as abnormal unless they are helped to understand that wide variations are possible in normal growth and development. With adolescence come new powers of reasoning and skill, and developing needs for social and moral understanding, personal identity and the security of close relationships and a vocational role. At this stage of their development young people need support, guidance and adult models.

The ability to recognize and respond to these stages of development is part of a teacher's essential armoury. Effective education depends more on developmental than chronological age.

Problem two: identifying obstacles

Teachers know, in their bones, the importance of the distinction between developmental and chronological age. But they may sometimes forget the obstacles they have to overcome to match curriculum and teaching to developmental age. As Brierley observes: 'Age of admission to school, age of transfer from one school to another, age of leaving, classification by IQ and examinations, the type of curriculum, are all mainly based on chronological age.'[2]

This is one of the most serious obstacles to providing each child with an effective curriculum. Teachers need to identify what other obstacles may prevent their delivering a curriculum which matches their aspirations. Then they must either remove or bypass the obstacles, or modify their aspirations.

The obstacles vary from school to school. For some parental and public opinion may be a problem. Every school has to be sensitive to public opinion, and to parental opinion generally, as well as to individual parents. Schools need time and skill to negotiate both the terms of reference which underpin their curricular thinking and the particular programmes of individual pupils.

A school's curricular thinkers need to consider also their colleagues. Not all are equally enlightened or equally energetic. What a school can achieve will depend on understanding, commitment and energy.

It may depend also on colleagues to rethink some element of a school's organization, rules and relationships.

The way teachers talk to each other, the way they talk to pupils and their accessibility to pupils, the school's policies on matters like streaming and examination entries, the school's rules and how they are enforced, even the timetable, all contribute to what is often called the hidden curriculum.

This curriculum consists of the values and attitudes implied by a school's organization and relationships. There is no more difficult task than trying to ensure that what a school does is compatible with what it seeks to achieve.

One specific obstacle merits a separate mention. External examinations provide a target for most secondary-school pupils. Success in the examinations is highly prized by parents and pupils because it is the way to further education and employment. Since teachers naturally wish their pupils to succeed, the examinations influence both what is taught and how it is taught, and the values implied by the examination system spread through the schools. These values may be exactly what a school wishes to pursue. Particularly by using Mode III examinations teachers have been able to match their own curricular thinking and the examination system. It is nonetheless a major constraint in planning the curriculum.

Problem three: organizing the planning

Schools are not alone in having difficult organizational problems. Among its parents, governors and friends a school may have people with experience of organizing other kinds of work. This experience might be harnessed by a school, perhaps in the way suggested on p. 33.

One common solution to organizational problems has been to manage different aspects of an organization's work in different ways. The army has, for example, a director of recruiting equal in rank to the director of engineering and to the general commanding each region. Many manufacturing and commercial organizations have, similarly, a director of personnel, a director of finance, and store or factory managers. In each of these examples some people have responsibilities for particular tasks like recruiting or personnel work, others for specialist services like engineering or accounting, and others for activities on a particular site.

Analysis of a school's organizational problems sometimes points to a similar solution. Some teachers may be responsible for integrating the work of a class or year group, others for organizing an aspect of the curriculum throughout a school, and others for supervising the use of a group of buildings. Blending the contributions of those with different kinds of responsibilities is one of the head's most demanding tasks.

Her Majesty's Inspectors' primary survey pointed out how rare it is for primary teachers with a special responsibility to exercise it effectively. About three quarters had little influence, and only one in twenty had a strong influence, as Table 1 shows. But, they said, 'where a teacher with a special responsibility was able to exercise it through the planning and supervision of a programme of work, this was effective in raising the standards of work and the levels of expectation of what children were capable of doing'.[3]

Table 1 Percentage of teachers with posts of responsibility in primary schools having strong, some or little influence

Class	Strong influence	Some influence	Little influence	Total
7 year olds	6	21	73	100
9 year olds	5	19	76	100
11 year olds	4	19	77	100

Source: Adapted from Department of Education and Science, *Primary education in England*, HMSO, 1978, pp. 105–6.

Many of these posts in primary schools carry responsibility for language work, mathematics or science. It is important to ensure that their skills influence their colleagues.

In most secondary schools there is a head of department in each of the main subjects, and he or she does usually co-ordinate the work in that subject. But secondary schools run into trouble in achieving some of their cross-curricular aims. Some will wish to develop programmes of health or social and personal education through several subjects. Others have similar aims in language and communication skills, library and study skills, environmental education, preparation for working life and understanding technology. In each of these and many other areas there are problems of leadership and co-ordination. Similar problems arise in integrating the different strands of one pupil's or one form's work.

In these circumstances, Her Majesty's Inspectors' secondary survey said:

Teachers need a view of the school curriculum as a whole and the part they are playing in it if they are to co-ordinate their pupils' learning and provide them with some sense of coherence in their programmes ... Pupils need a range of experiences which in practice is provided through the subjects in the timetable. But if these subjects are to contribute more effectively to the broad education of the pupils many specialist teachers will have to break away from the isolation in which they commonly work.[4]

They need to develop for their own use the skills in group work which are said to be important in industry and commerce.

The primary survey shows how difficult this has been. HMI thought that children's work benefited only when the responsible teachers planned and supervised agreed programmes of work. Assigning a responsibility has no value in itself, unless the teacher to whom responsibility is assigned exercises a strong lead in planning and carrying out programmes.

Though our minds turn readily to identifying leaders, it seems worth asking whether this is the best reply to the evidence of the primary survey. The best way forward may be in asking one person to activate the work of a group charged with an important task. In a primary school the group may be the whole staff activated at one task by one of its specialist members and at other tasks by other members.

This sort of approach may be very helpful now opportunities for promotion are much restricted. There are more jobs to be done than people to do them. A seven-class primary school, for example, might want to develop conscious policies on language and communication, number work, art and craft, music, science, history and geography, physical education, personal and social development, and other matters too. There is clearly an opportunity for each teacher in such a school to make a distinctive contribution as the school's specialist in at least one aspect of the curriculum.

Whatever a school's size, it has to identify the need for policies and plans, and decide who is to be responsible for working out policy and turning it into effective action.

A small school has the same educational aims and the same tasks as a large one, so the teachers in a small school are more likely to be asked to wear several specialist hats. In larger schools it may be possible to ask an experienced teacher to make a small and clearly defined area such as group work, problem-solving or study skills his or her main specialism. Such a teacher could elicit the help of other teachers with different subject specialisms and teaching pupils of different ages, to work out an overall strategy for the school.

Whatever approach a school adopts to planning and co-ordination it will need to ask how it will decide whether those responsible are having a significant and helpful impact on the pupils' work.

Problem four: talking about the curriculum

Measuring success, like planning a curriculum and agreeing aims, requires a professional language. In the first instance a simple language to describe the curriculum would be useful.

Building on earlier work by some of Her Majesty's Inspectors, Brian Wilcox and Peter Eustace have described such a language in their book *Tooling up for Curriculum Review.*[5] This describes a system of notation which enables its users to state the curriculum of even a large and complex school in a clear, straightforward way.

The system provides an at-a-glance guide to the subjects offered to different groups of pupils in a school, the number of teaching periods allocated to each subject, the balance of subjects within the curriculum and the organization of teaching groups.

A summary like this provides the background for deeper discussion between teachers, between teachers and governors, between school and local authority. It is a useful starting point for planning change in the curriculum, and a good basis for comparing what is happening in several schools and in a whole local authority.

Many local authorities are beginning to use this system, or one derived from it, to improve their own knowledge of the curricula their schools offer. Even if the local authority does not require its use, we believe every school would find it helpful to adopt a system like this. And although Brian Wilcox and Peter Eustace were concerned with ways of describing secondary schools' curricula, we believe their methods might be helpful also to junior and middle schools.

Another possible extension of the system would be to use it to describe each pupil's curriculum. In schools with numerous options, form tutors might find the notation a useful means of recording the actual curriculum of each of their pupils.

The system we have referred to is a *simple way of describing the pattern of subjects a school offers*. It does not attempt to describe the modes of teaching and learning teachers use, nor the values, attitudes, understanding and skills they hope their pupils will acquire. The teachers in each school need a professional language to talk about what happens in the classroom and the skills their pupils are acquiring. Developing this kind of professional competence will not be easy. *It might perhaps be helpful if teachers were encouraged to make professional reports to their colleagues on various aspects of learning*. This could be the means of developing both a common language and greater self-awareness.

Problem five: making a start

'It's not what you do but the way that you do it,' said the songwriter. We know our pupils learn some things well by doing them, and some things cannot be learned in any other way.

So it is with planning and talking about the curriculum. We all learn how to do things by doing them, and *schools will learn how to plan and how to talk about the curriculum by making a start*.

The head of one school described their start in this way.

In January, 1978, I circulated a review of our 11–16 curriculum which consisted of questions about aims, balance and suitability. After thorough discussion of this document we felt we could only proceed if all the staff were willing to be involved. We therefore decided to mount a one-day conference. Participants at the Hull College of Education (our hosts) included our staff, advisers (who had already taken part in departmental discussions), governors, heads of contributory primary schools, parents, and representatives of industry, the Schools Council and HM Inspectorate.

The conference proved a great success. Our two speakers represented very different views which excited voluble and varied reaction. Afterwards, all bar one of our staff of 92 indicated that they wanted to take part in continuing discussions. Groups were established to air the following subjects:

1. aims   2. classification and design   3. distribution   4. pupil organisation   5. staff organisation   6. teaching methods   7. pupil evaluation   8. staff evaluation.

After discussion on Aims a report was circulated for comment, and a meeting of the Parent–Staff Association was called to discuss the findings. Almost 200 parents came to the meeting, an astonishing number, and their group discussion was both revealing and constructive.

At present, discussion groups have produced reports on the first four topics while Staff Organisation and Teaching Methods are under active review.

To date, although behind schedule, we can be pleased with our progress. The lessons we have learned are:

1. Full staff participation is necessary
2. A staff conference with the stimulus of guest speakers is an excellent way of sparking off initial discussion
3. Participation of a wide spectrum of those concerned with education is important
4. The local authority must recognise that this kind of operation, in which teachers are asked to give up additional free time, has to be funded. Fortunately, County Humberside paid for our conference and also gave us money to employ supply staff to replace teachers meeting in school time. Additionally, teachers meeting in the evening were paid a transport allowance
5. Discussion groups are best organised not in accordance with the patterns of school organisation (academic departments or pastoral groups) but by voluntary interest, chairmen being chosen by reason of their experience and breadth of vision
6. Those involved in discussion should be willing to read the supporting literature prepared
7. Discussions should be built into a schedule so that reports appear regularly and can be distributed for comment.[6]

This school also reviewed its provision for slow learners, and came up with thoughts for training staff and improving the resources for slow learners.

1. Mixed-ability grouping was demanding on staff expertise and school resources.

2. In-school training was needed in preparing worksheets and other material for the less able.
3. The LEA might provide opportunities for in-service training in mixed-ability teaching.
4. The expertise of teachers with training in remedial education, language and number teaching should be used in the training of subject teachers.
5. Improved libraries and other non-book materials were essential, especially for non-examination work.
6. An expanded reprographic department was needed, with more help in collation, counting, stapling and punching worksheets. A higher quality of graphics and presentation was needed and absolute priority given to production of a final item which could be used by the teacher. Possible volunteer parent help should be extended to this task.

This example does not explain whether the suggestions were put into practice. After review and recommendations come planning for change, and change itself. The Schools Council's Health Education Project suggested the following stages in developing a new programme of personal education:

1. A commited head forms a small and powerful steering committee and asks a senior colleague to lead the committee.
2. The committee clear their minds, and describe what they understand by personal education, why it is needed and what the school already does.
3. Their statement is used to stimulate discussion with colleagues, parents, pupils and local community. The committee intends this discussion to promote understanding and agreement on aims.
4. The committee establishes what resources are available to achieve the new policy.
5. Further discussion secures agreement on what is to be done.
6. Plans are made and put into effect.
7. The steering committee asks what has been achieved and whether it matches the agreed aims.[7]

In planning the curriculum, as in much that schools do for their pupils, experience and reflection are the best teachers. No school should be cast down if its first efforts seem rough and unpolished.

Problem six: resources, or money for men, machines and materials

The school mentioned in the previous section needed money for running a conference and paying supply teachers. Later it needed money for training, improved libraries and non-book materials and an enlarged and better-staffed reprographic department. The Health Education Project identified the problem of providing resources to implement a new policy.

In each case the problem was to find the resources to implement a desired policy. Securing a match between agreed curriculum policies and the resources to fund these policies has been recognized only recently as a central issue in educational planning. The reason it was not recognized earlier lies in the way resources are provided for schools. Most local authorities allocate resources in accordance with simple rationing systems, based mainly on the number and age of a school's pupils. One system is used to calculate the number of teachers each school may have, another the number of non-teaching staff and a third the amount of money a school may spend on small equipment, books and materials. Knowing their resources, schools then shape their curricular policies and plans accordingly.

The system means that large schools are able to offer more variations than small schools. This was recognized in the early days of comprehensive schools, when both friend and foe argued that a comprehensive school needed eight or ten forms in each age group to be able to offer all the variations such a school should offer. Many authorities have had similar debates about the right size for middle or junior schools.

Almost always the question has been put at least implicitly in this way: given the way in which resources are allocated, how large do schools need to be to have a reasonable amount of specialist accommodation and equipment, a reasonable spread of specialist teachers and a reasonable variety in their curriculum?

The threat of falling numbers has turned this question back to front. If it is appropriate to stream the pupils in a ten-form-entry school, to offer the possibility of studying physics, chemistry and biology as separate subjects and the possibility of studying two or three foreign languages, and to offer a wide choice of courses for 14- and 15-year-old pupils, is it reasonable to withdraw these facilities when the school's numbers fall, perhaps by half in a few years?

In *Falling Rolls in Secondary Schools* Eric Briault and Frances Smith have shown how schools behave when their numbers fall. They increase the average size of classes in a year group or in basic subjects, reduce the amount of small-group work, reduce the number of optional subjects, extend the range of ability in each class, cut the second or third foreign language and reduce the possibility of taking the three sciences as separate subjects. If a specialist teacher leaves they may have to redeploy someone with another subject specialism. The effect of falling rolls, in primary as well as secondary schools, has been to highlight the inadequacy of most existing systems for allocating resources to schools. 'It is clear,' say Briault and Smith, 'that an overall pupil/teacher ratio applied to a total number of pupils of statutory school age is an extremely blunt instrument.'[8]

How blunt may be seen by imagining a secondary school using the outline curriculum illustrated on p. 39 below. The timetable has two elements, the common curriculum offered to all pupils, and certain options mentioned in the text.

If the imaginary 11–16 school had one form of thirty pupils in each age group the number of teaching periods required for the curriculum would be 200 divided as follows:

$$E_{23} \; M_{23} \; S_{40} \; Ss_{26} \; La_{20} \; RE_3 \; Mu_3 \; ACrDTkHk_{34} \; PE/Ga_{20} \; Courses_8.$$

200 teaching periods would require the equivalent of six teachers if each taught thirty-two or thirty-three periods in a forty-period week. To maintain the options would require eight more periods of science, eight of social studies, eight of modern languages, four of English and four of mathematics, a total of thirty-two periods, requiring one more teacher. The actual cost of maintaining these options would be exactly the same in larger schools, that is one extra teacher, provided the number choosing an alternative was not so large that extra sets were required.

The cost of maintaining certain options is therefore less relatively in larger schools. As a survey of schools in sparsely populated areas showed, small schools need more teachers, relatively, than large schools to be able to offer the same curriculum.[9] A curriculum which included fewer options and small groups would reduce the differences between large and small schools, but would be more vulnerable to the loss of key members of staff.

Another largely unpublicized difficulty arises from the practice of teaching some subjects to classes of thirty and other practical subjects to classes of no more than twenty. Of the 200 periods in our one-form-entry school, seventy-four in science, art, craft, design, technology and home economics would probably be taught in classes of twenty or less. In these circumstances schools whose entry in each age group is neatly divisible by both thirty and twenty are able to use their staff and accommodation more economically than others.

Other schools, particularly old primary schools, sometimes find that the size and shape of their rooms forces them to run a number of small classes which they would not justify on purely educational grounds. This may take teacher time which could be used in other schools for small-group work or specialist support.

Teachers also have to consider what equipment and materials they need to achieve their curricular aims. In formulating a school policy for science, for example, primary teachers need to consider what materials and apparatus they need for

   i arousing and maintaining children's curiosity
   ii making collections of specimens and data
  iii maintaining materials in living and preserved states
  iv developing inquiry skills
   v promoting the scientific aspects of interdisciplinary studies
  vi aiding communication
 vii gaining experience at second hand.

They have to plan and organize buying, collecting, storing, maintaining and caring for specialist equipment and materials. The needs are the same whatever the size of the school.

Since these examples show beyond doubt that equal shares must mean unequal provision for the pupils, we believe it is time to agree on a guaranteed curricular offer to every pupil. Starting from the need to make such an offer each school, its governors and its local authority could calculate what resources were required, in the unique circumstances of each school, to provide that entitlement. Educational opportunity should not depend on the vagaries of local variations in the number of children or other accidents of history.

Planning in action

In a recent report on the Schools Council's Language Across the Curriculum Project, Irene Robertson illustrates how four schools tackled some of these planning problems.[10] One established a Language Policy Committee of teachers and pupils, and another invited each department to nominate a member of a Language and Learning Committee. Members recognized that they did not know what went on in lessons other than their own, and the committee arranged for pupils' activities, and their views, to be monitored. Talking about the use of language led several teachers to a deeper appreciation of what teaching their own subject meant. A teacher of physical education came to see the importance of clarity in his instructions, and of letting pupils take over a problem. A metalwork teacher displayed lists of specialist metalworking words and others which cropped up frequently in metalwork lessons. The English and science departments recognized a common interest in helping their pupils to use their senses in close observation and identified topics including natural life, natural habitat, safety, food and transport where the work of the two departments could be linked. Other departments, from mathematics to history and drama, also contributed time and energy to working out a coherent strategy for developing language across the curriculum.

Another school which was equally successful in stimulating interest in language development in several departments was able to benefit from the work of a local co-ordinator working in several schools, sharing experiences with teachers in other schools, and specialist courses in particular subjects. These activities take time and energy and are an integral part of teachers' personal and professional development. Based at school or at local centres, they need not be expensive, but local authorities must recognize that effective teaching demands investment in these forms of professional development.

Problem seven: making a timetable

In Chapter I we discussed several ways of looking at the curriculum, through the underlying principles on which it rests, its aims, the kinds of knowledge and experience it opens up, the modes of teaching and learning it uses, the values and attitudes, and the skills and capacity for self-expression it seeks to develop.

The problem for practising teachers is to translate their thoughts on these matters into a realizable programme for their pupils. In most schools the last stage in this process is making a timetable, or at least deciding on a programme of activities for their pupils.

Children at nursery and infant schools usually enjoy a flexible programme of activities, carefully chosen to encourage exploration, observation, communication and number skills. Teachers of older children gradually introduce more formal distinctions between subjects and a more formal timetable. By the time they reach 13 most pupils have a structured timetable of subjects.

The challenge for all schools is to ensure that these activities and subjects are an adequate vehicle for realizing their curricular ideas. 'Most school subjects, imaginatively handled,' the Secretaries of State said in *A framework for the school curriculum*, 'can contribute to the achievement of many – perhaps all – of the general aims' they had described.[11]

The first task in importance is to tease out what contribution each activity and each subject could make and what contribution it can make in the particular circumstances of each school. That task needs to be undertaken as part of the larger process of deciding what activities or subjects a school is to offer, and what each pupil is to study. For the pupils it is not so much the range and the choices offered but what is provided within that range for each pupil that is more important.

A familiar subject label may cover diverse aims and diverse kinds of interaction between pupil and teacher. This means that it is not particularly helpful to describe a curriculum only in terms of subjects. They are simply the vehicles for teaching and learning. Despite this, secondary schools and some primary schools do find it helpful to use a subject timetable as a shorthand description of their curriculum.

About twenty subject titles would be enough to describe most of the curriculum in most schools. They would include:

        1 English
        2 Mathematics
    3, 4, 5 Science (including Nature Study, Biology, Chemistry and Physics)
  6, 7, 8, 9 Social Studies (including Environmental Studies, Geography, History, Politics and Economics)
     10, 11 Foreign Languages
        12 Religious Education
        13 Music
        14 Art
        15 Craft
        16 Design
        17 Technology
        18 Home Economics
 19, 20, 21 Physical Education (including Athletics, Swimming, Gymnastics and Dance), Games and Outdoor Pursuits
        22 Careers Education
        23 Short courses

Particularly for older pupils some schools may also include a programme of short courses in subjects such as computer studies, consumer education, childcare, community service and work experience. A programme of short courses might also sometimes include some of the twenty-two subjects listed above.

We have used this list of subjects to construct the outline timetable shown in Table 2. It illustrates one way of maintaining a broad common

Table 2

Age of pupils	1 E	2 M	3 Nature Study	4 General Science / Biology	5 Chemistry / Physics	6 Environmental Studies	7 Social Studies	8 History / Geography	9 Politics & Economics	10 LA¹	11 LA²	12 RE	13 Mu	14 A	15 Cr	16 D	17 Tk	18 Hk	19 PE	20 Ga	21 Ou	22 Ca	23 Short courses
5	E	M	NS			Ev						RE	Mu	A	Cr				PE	Ga			
6	E	M	NS			Ev						RE	Mu	A	Cr				PE	Ga			
7	E	M	NS			Ev						RE	Mu	A	Cr				PE	Ga			
8	E	M		S			from Ss/H/G					RE	Mu	A	Cr			Hk	PE	Ga			
9	E	M		S			from Ss/H/G					RE	Mu	A	Cr	from	Tk	Hk	PE	Ga			
10	E	M		S			Ss/H/G					RE	Mu	A	Cr	D	Tk	Hk	PE	Ga			
11	E₅	M₅			S₈		SOCIAL STUDIES₆ or H or G			La₄		RE₁	Mu₁	A	Cr	D	Tk	Hk₆	PE₂	Ga₂			
12	E₅	M₅			S₈		SOCIAL STUDIES₆ or H or G			La₄		RE₁	Mu₁	*a programme including* Cr	D	Tk	Hk₆	PE₂	Ga₂				
13	E₅	M₅			S₈		SOCIAL STUDIES₆ or H or G			La₄		RE₁	Mu₁	A	Cr	D	Tk	Hk₆	PE₂	Ga₂			
14	E₄	M₄			S₈		Ss or H or G₄			La₄		*	*	2 from A,	Cr,	D,	Tk,	Hk₈	PE/Ga/Ou₄				*
15	E₄	M₄			S₈		Ss or H or G₄			La₄		*	*	2 from A,	Cr,	D,	Tk,	Hk₈	PE/Ga/Ou₄				*

curriculum for all pupils up to 16, but we have included it here only as a basis for discussion. Comparing it with a school's existing timetable may stimulate helpful analysis, or highlight some important issues.

Primary schools usually have a more flexible timetable than secondary schools, and a more integrated approach. In that context it does not seem sensible to talk of allocating periods to subjects. For pupils of 11 and over, a forty-period week is assumed. Pupils of 14 and 15 are shown with a timetable consisting of ten blocks of four periods each. They take eight examinable subjects, four periods each, with four periods for Physical Education and Games, and four periods for courses in Politics and Economics, Religious Education, Music, Craft or Home Economics and Careers, and other short courses. Some pupils might take an additional science, a second social study or a second foreign language, instead of taking a second subject from the group consisting of Art, CDT and Home Economics. Others might do additional work in English or Mathematics instead of taking a foreign language.

Where to find help

Apart from learning by doing, schools have other strategies for developing their skills. They may themselves be able to organize a few staff seminars, and fund the purchase of a few well-chosen books.

Judicious use of some outside courses in management, organizational development or interpersonal relations may pay dividends. Another possibility is to import help from outside such as an HMI, LEA adviser or lecturer from a university, polytechnic or institute of higher education.

The Schools Council may sometimes be able to help schools or groups of schools which wish to go this way. Helping teachers to develop their professional skills and helping schools to grapple with the problems of purpose and planning are two of our five major concerns, and we have some funds available to support local activities with these aims.

Checkpoints for action

1. Has a teacher agreed to accept responsibility for planning to achieve each of the aims the school has set itself?
2. Has the school identified the obstacles which stand in its way, and decided how to deal with each of them?
3. Have appropriate people agreed how they will decide whether the curriculum matches their pupils' development and whether this planning is having a helpful impact on the pupils' work?

4. Has the school adopted effective ways of describing what actually happens in its classrooms?
5. What strategies has the school used in the last year to develop its skills in planning, discussing and reviewing its curriculum?
6. Precisely what resources are necessary to maintain the agreed curriculum?
7. Have the governors and LEA discussed resources in relation to a guaranteed curricular entitlement?
8. Will the proposed timetable enable the school to achieve its aims?

III. Monitoring the curriculum

Our first two chapters were about guiding principles and aims, and planning what is to be done in order to achieve what a school wants to happen. This chapter is about finding out what is being done, and checking whether it is consistent with plans, principles and aims.

We suggest several ways in which teachers can monitor what their school is doing. This is an important and necessary task. It is rather like taking an invalid's temperature or checking tyre pressures and oil levels, a thing to be done carefully, from time to time, as the prelude to assessment and review. Our suggestions are tentative because the art of monitoring a school's curriculum is still in its developmental phase.

In the first instance teachers, head and governors need to satisfy themselves that their school has worked out a rationale for its curriculum and is using terms of reference like those we described in Chapter I. They will wish to know what the school is doing to organize its planning, to talk about the curriculum, to learn from its own experience and to match resources and policies.

In this chapter we start with a pupil's view of the curriculum. Then we suggest how teachers might monitor the content of the curriculum, the allocation of time to various parts of the curriculum and continuity and progression in their pupils' work. In all this the most important question is whether schools and teachers are monitoring their pupils' experiences and relating these to the school's aims. We end the chapter by suggesting ways of checking whether this is happening.

A pupil's view of the curriculum

For the children themselves the effective curriculum is what each child takes away. *Schools and their teachers need ways of finding out what each child's experience is* and how well they are learning what the school intends. This is a more difficult task in secondary than in primary schools. Class

42

teachers in primary or secondary schools are well placed to take an over-view of each pupil's experience and help the pupil to assess it. Specialist teaching and the typically fractured day of secondary schools make it a great deal harder for most secondary teachers to do this.

A form tutor may have a good overview of the experience his or her colleagues have planned; with sympathetic imagination a tutor may feel what the pupils experience. But there seems to be no substitute for sharing their experience, seeing the day as the pupils see it and listening to what they say about it. A report from the Welsh Office commented:

Following a group of pupils through a day in a secondary school has revealed that their language experiences are largely a matter of chance. The dominant modes are expositions by teachers, questions and answers, the writing of notes and answers to work-sheets. The pupils' own use of language oral and written may be subject only to spasmodic correction of superficial features. It is not unusual to find classes of below-average pupils spending several lessons during a particular day neatly copying out passages from books which they cannot read with understanding, when they are unable to write in clear, acceptable language a simple account of what they have learned. The failure to provide adequate opportunities for such pupils through discussion to develop their use of language and come to an understanding of the concepts used in particular subjects denies them the incentive to participate and the confidence to progress in their learning.[1]

Her Majesty's Inspectors made a similar point in their report on secondary education. When HMI followed groups of pupils for a day, they found too much reading and writing and too little discussion.

One headteacher who checked what was happening in his own school found that one form was given workcards in one lesson after another throughout the day. He had to ask whether it was sensible either to use them to that extent, or to exclude other methods of learning.

Similar checks on the experience of particular pupils may also be illuminating. One class of 10-year-olds studying their local community had an exciting series of lessons with visitors coming in to talk about their jobs. There were many opportunities for role play and much good work was done. Only afterwards did the teacher realize that one boy had first been asked to play the role of a heavily bandaged patient on a stretcher, then a member of a jury, then . . . all essentially non-speaking roles. By accident it seemed he had been denied access to rich areas of experience.

In another school one of the heads of department observed and recorded a pupil's activities during a typical thirty-minute lesson. The pupil spent most of the first sixteen minutes listening and observing, and the last four-teen minutes considering decisions and writing and sometimes talking. He sat throughout the lesson, but was often moving in the second part of the lesson. He was visibly inattentive quite often in the first part of the lesson while the teacher was explaining the lesson's purpose and plan, but was attentive in the second part.

A different approach to portraying a school day as one boy saw it was adopted in a slide–tape sequence. In this the photographer was at pains to get into the boy's skin, to see the day as he saw it, whereas most of our examples illustrate ways of recording and analysing a pupil's or form's activities.

Irene Robertson's report *Language across the curriculum* illustrates how four schools monitored their attempts to develop across-the-board work in language development. In one school two teachers each followed a pupil for a day to observe and report on the pupil's language experience, and pupils kept diaries of a week's lessons. 'This lesson is good,' wrote one, 'because you have to work on your own and ask your own questions.' Another wrote, 'I find it is so frustrating when the teacher spends half the lesson explaining it to you and you still don't understand. But when I finally did understand it is so simple. Then when a girl has been away I explained it to her and it only took me about two minutes and she understood.'

In another school teachers collected a year's exercise books from six pupils, and found that of 203 275 words in them 95 525 had been copied or dictated. To their surprise they found also that for these pupils some other subjects involved more writing than English.

In a third school a survey showed what proportion of their time pupils spent on various activities. Both teachers and pupils reported much teacher talking and little discussion, but otherwise there were marked differences between what pupils thought was happening and what teachers thought.

In that school a teacher of physical education tape-recorded his lessons so that he could monitor such matters as how questioning was used, how pupils were informed of their successes, how misunderstandings occurred and were dealt with, and the extent to which the language used in gymnastics and in dance was similar or different. In answering these questions he was able to visualize how the lessons looked to the pupils.[2]

These examples are merely illustrative. Teachers will readily invent their own ways of monitoring their pupils' activities and seeing school as the pupils see it.

Analysing content

The subject labels on school timetables give the timetables a marked family likeness to each other. This appearance is sometimes deceptive. The subject labels may cover a range of content, experience and outcomes.

On their own, subject titles say little about what is taught or what is learned in schools. Syllabuses add something, but may say little about what teachers and pupils are going to do, or what values, attitudes, skills and understanding teachers hope their pupils will acquire.

Detailed schemes of work might fill these gaps. Such a scheme might

provide a written programme of study

suggest ways of approaching that content

suggest appropriate learning strategies and materials

indicate appropriate materials, resources and study skills, perhaps with a commentary on different uses

outline appropriate pupil assessment procedures

propose sample assignments

contain statements about how these learning experiences fit into the overall context of the school

indicate how the course as a whole is to be monitored.

Teachers are most likely to have such detailed schemes for individual subjects. What might be interesting, useful and practicable now would be to prepare such schemes for a single form or year group, perhaps in the first instance for a related group of subjects, or to illustrate how several subjects contribute to certain cross-curricular themes.

The Schools Council's own work in careers education led us to think about the contribution various subjects could make. We found that a dozen of our own projects had produced relevant materials. Among them were a resource pack on People and Work from the Humanities Project, units on Industry and Urban Geography from Geography 14–18, and units on applying for a job and negotiation at work from Language in Use. Personal development and self-awareness are important themes in our Health Education, Moral Education and Drama Projects. Knowledge of modern society is one of the themes of our work in General Studies and in History, Geography and Social Science. Other work in Mathematics, Science and Technology has shown how their general principles can be illuminated by practical examples from current industrial practice, so that work in these subjects too can contribute to careers education.

Another of the Council's leaflets shows the contribution science, geography, history, social studies, technology, mathematics, art and many others can make to environmental education.

This is illustrated very effectively in the following notes of how one school orchestrates the work of several departments in a study of population growth.

Mathematics	exponential increase, graphical representation, statistical forecasting
History	past limitations on growth (emigration, disease, famine, war)
Geography	population distribution, natural controls (climate, soil fertility, water supply)
Economics	affluence and family size, state social support, education (literacy, statutory age)
Religious/ Social Studies	world organization (WHO, UNICEF), social custom (infanticide, marriage age, killing of widows), political (genocide, sterilization, laws), sectarian (attitude to birth control)
Science, Biology, Rural Studies	population dynamics (yeast experiments, plant dispersal), mammalian reproduction (abortion, contraception), ecological balance (predators, natural selection), pest control, modern medicine (antisepsis, organ transplants), water purification (sanitation, sewage disposal).[3]

In preparing and using schemes of work teachers face the familiar problem of ensuring that knowledge is translated into good practice. The light-hearted extract which follows is a cautionary tale. It illustrates the satirical view of a newly appointed management-oriented head.

After assembly I went through the replies from the staff to my role-assessment questionnaire. Arnold Bogwin, my deputy, brought in what there was of them – most had mysteriously gone astray. One of the key questions was, 'Please specify the teaching objectives of your last lesson,' and there were some odd replies. One of the scientists had submitted a long list starting with 'Get pupils to light bunsens. Check whether all are alight. Issue safety masks and ensure radioactive cupboard locked. Wheel in the trolley, checking the door firmly closed beyond,' and so on for three pages. But one of the English staff had just written, 'Unlocking the treasure-house of literature.' It's amazing that people can answer a simple question so differently. According to Arnold, the English person is one of our best teachers, which I found rather surprising.[4]

These schemes of work should enable teachers to

i identify what themes and topics are being covered, where and when;
ii explore differences between the stated aims and how these aims are interpreted in teaching;
iii decide whether any overlap between the schemes for different subjects is desirable.

If schemes like these were collected they could form the agenda for a valuable staff discussion about what the pupils in a form or year actually study. Such schemes would illustrate different approaches to learning. They would also help the teachers taking part to ensure that they made use of an interesting range of different courses.

It may be helpful also to bring out the ways in which subjects depend on each other. One analysis of this sort showed the links between a GCE A-level syllabus in mathematics and its application in other subjects. A knowledge of indices and standard form was either essential or highly desirable in biology, chemistry, physics, economics and sociology, and desirable in geography. Knowledge of the χ^2 test was essential in biology, physics, geography and sociology and highly desirable in psychology. But only biology and economics needed any knowledge of linear programming.[5]

Once a school had decided its cross-curricular aims, each teaching team might be asked to confirm whether they already contribute to achieving an aim, and to say whether they could contribute more by modifying their syllabus.

If a course can contribute significantly to an important theme teachers will need to know whether the course is compulsory for all pupils or optional. If the course is optional they will need to ask whether pupils who opt out have any other opportunity of achieving the same aims.

The problem of time

The aims of education are the same for all children, but the time they spend on the journey may vary greatly. The maximum length of their school life depends on their birthday, and the length of the school year depends on where they live.

Children who reach 16 between September and February may leave at the following Easter, after more than eleven years at school, whereas those who reach 16 between May and August may leave before their sixteenth birthday. The effect is that even among those leaving at the first opportunity some will spend two terms more at school than others.

These differences are matched by differences in the length of the school year. These can amount to 150 hours a year, a range of nearly 20 per cent between the highest and lowest comprehensive school. The effect of these differences is multiplied by similar differences in the amount of homework set. Even without the further differences caused by ill-health or absence, some children spend about 30 per cent more time than others do on school work.

These disparities highlight the need to make effective use of the time children spend at school. One important preliminary step is to find out exactly how the time available for learning is spent.

The most straightforward questions are about the way a school allocates time to different subjects. Schools may find it helpful to compare their own practice with the suggestions in *A framework for the school curriculum.* The Department of Education and Science suggested there that children should spend at least 10 per cent of their time on English, at least 10 per cent on mathematics, between 10 and 20 per cent on science, and about 10 per cent for at least two years on a foreign language. These proportions were not related to the length of the school year, though variations in the time children spend at school are among the reasons why schools might allocate different proportions of time to each subject.[6]

In addition to considering the DES recommendations schools may want to check their allocation of time to other subjects. These allocations will not necessarily be the same for each age group, and need not necessarily be the same throughout a school year. Even within a single school it might be worth asking whether pupils of every age are best served by the same length and pattern of school day.

Many schools faced with the prospect of falling rolls may find it helpful to consider the issues raised in Weston's case study of a school with a rapidly changing age profile. She wondered whether this provides an opportunity

to look again at the characteristics of the timetable framework itself, and the units from which it is constructed? Perhaps the fact that there were no younger pupils in the school might contribute to new thinking about the units of time appropriate for work, as well as the possible varieties of pupil grouping. And how should the framework be adapted to express the fact that for the majority the 'third year' in this context would be the foundation of a course limited to three years? ... Certainly it is worth remembering that it was in some of the well-established comprehensive schools in our sample that moves towards a more 'open' modular timetabling system had been made.[7]

Though Weston saw a change in the school's age profile as the opportunity for reconsidering what units of time were appropriate, schools could ask this question at other times too. One health education project being tested in certain middle schools depends on immersing the children in the project for about half their time for several weeks. Similarly, adult students of modern languages often make remarkable progress by learning in this way. The practice of partial or total immersion for short periods may be preferable, sometimes and for some purposes, to the steady drip theory on which most school timetables seem to be planned.

Issues like this involve judgements about the effective use of time. This depends partly on the various kinds of learning experience pupils have. Schools may need ways of finding out how much of their time pupils spend working on their own or working in groups, how much time they spend using banks of resources or solving problems, or how much time they spend on any other kind of activity.

A class teacher or a team of teachers might adopt the practice sometimes used in surveys of administrative and executive work of noting how much time they spend on one or more agreed activities. Class teachers might find this a useful way of checking whether they are achieving a sensible balance between the various styles of teaching in their armoury. Teams of teachers may use it as a way of ensuring that they achieve an overall balance and provide their pupils with varied learning experiences.

Another way to monitor the use of time is to record pupils' learning experiences over a given period of, say, a week. One school did this and found that pupils spent 32 per cent of their time writing, 30 per cent listening, 10 per cent speaking, 10 per cent reading and 18 per cent thinking.

Schools might also ask their pupils to keep a note of their own activities. This would be a useful exercise for the pupils, as well as providing valuable information for the staff.

Table 3 illustrates an interesting attempt to compare a teacher's analysis of his activities in one lesson with a pupil's analysis of the same lesson.

Table 3

Teacher activities as viewed by the teacher	%	Pupil's activity as viewed by herself	%
Transmitting information	43	Taking notes	35
Individual tutoring	16	Listening	36
Writing	10	Discussion:	
Supervising	6		
Administration	3	with other pupils	18
Discussion	22	with teacher	11
	100		100

Note: No reading activity was planned for the lesson.
Source: Internal working party document, Carisbrooke High School, Isle of Wight.

These examples of how some schools have tried to find out how teachers and pupils were spending their time show that this sort of inquiry need not be expensive or time-consuming. Quite simple and unsophisticated checks could provide teachers with valuable information and insights.

Continuity and progression

Analysing curriculum content and discovering how children spend their time are important means of monitoring the curriculum. More important still is to find out whether the various parts of a child's curriculum make a coherent whole, and whether the work becomes progressively more difficult in line with the child's development. If children can recognize the continuity in what they are taught and the progression in their own work, they will understand and value their curriculum.

Teachers who take one class for all or most of the time are well placed to ensure continuity and progression in their pupils' work. Teachers of young children especially can often give a powerful account of continuity in their pupils' education. They are able to relate their pupils' development to the educational experiences they have organized, the difficulty of the work, and current learning theory.

Teachers of older children are more likely to be subject specialists, teaching each class for only a fraction of the week. They are more likely to see continuity in terms of the subject content of their own specialism, because they have a necessarily limited knowledge of their pupils' personal development, or what else they are learning. 'We've done North America' or 'Henry IV' or 'the individual', such teachers may say, 'so we'll make a start on South America' or 'Henry V' or 'the family', or whatever the subject's logical framework suggests. This sort of scholarly framework implies some sort of continuity without there being any progression in the quality or difficulty of the pupils' work.

Some textbooks seem to be progressive but include so many repetitive exercises that at times the only element of progression lies in turning the pages. Bright pupils who finish one task quickly may be given another of about the same difficulty which they naturally find uninteresting.

Teachers in one authority have grappled with this problem by developing a set of continuity profiles. These show how the varied resources for mathematics in their schools could be used to provide opportunities for individualized learning (Secondary Mathematics Individualized Learning Experiment).[8] This experiment is intended to ensure continuity of learning experience for each child. It is intended also to ensure a steady advance in the quality of that experience and the work each child does. There is some assurance of progress as well as continuity of experience.

The teachers responsible for SMILE came to the conclusion that in mathematics at least their pupils needed to work individually if they were to make progress. If some children have to mark time while their slower peers catch up, so that new concepts can be introduced to a whole class at the same time, the work they do will not necessarily constitute progress.

Teachers concerned with this elusive concept of progress may also wish to explore questions about the relative merits of different pieces of work. At present there is little agreement about what is to be regarded as evidence on these matters. A history course in which pupils work through the kings of Portugal, or some other content based on a time series, certainly involves continuity of a sort, but does not necessarily involve progression.

The Schools Council Continuity and Development Project grappled with the problem of defining progression in social studies. Making systematic use of the local environment, teachers in Merton primary, middle and secondary schools identified key factors in each discipline and related these to the specific levels of understanding and skill that could be fostered at each stage of schooling. They hoped to ensure that in Merton schools children would, in social studies at least, follow fundamentally the same aims throughout their school years from 7 to 16, and would not have to start afresh each time they changed schools.[9]

Trying to ensure continuity and progression between one school and another, as these Merton teachers tried to do, is one of the most difficult problems. Recognizing exactly what constitutes progress in each subject is another. In some there is a measure of agreement about levels of difficulty, as the use of graded tests reveals. In others there is not much agreement about how to assess a pupil's level of understanding. In consequence there is little guidance about how to devise a progressive scheme of work which matches the pupil's stages of development.

The idea of progression is particularly elusive when several activities or subjects contribute to a general aim. Primary teachers have good opportunities for noticing their pupils' physical skills, their language and communication skills and their personal competence in many different contexts. They need infinite skill to piece these observations together to gain a coherent picture of their pupils' progression.

In secondary schools more formal procedures are needed. The following notes show how one school tries to secure progression in its work in environmental education.

First year: two full afternoons
1. Group Study – land, sea and air theme – whole year visits York
2. Integrated Study – geography, science, mathematics, traffic surveys, distribution surveys

Second year: one full week at country study centre – standard programme

Second and third years: field work, mostly local, especially in geography, history, science, film period

Fourth and   one full afternoon on course study – notion system gives each pupil
fifth year: ten units a year – community service, electricity and energy-saving
at home, conservation, plants of the world, urban trails, outdoor
pursuits, art history, civic pride, photography, local heritage, transport, radio and television communications, careers
option system includes environmental studies and geology
all pupils take science

Sixth and
seventh year: about one fifth of programme is assigned to general studies including science in society and environmental studies.[10]

This example illustrates also the contribution several subjects make to
environmental education. In that respect it typifies many of the most
important skills, values and kinds of understanding schools try to teach.
The problem of ensuring continuity and progression transcends subject
boundaries just as it transcends the boundaries between stages of schooling. Finding ways of monitoring continuity and progression would be one
of the best ways of providing children with an effective curriculum.

Matching aims and practice

Matching aims and practice is one of the big problems in any enterprise.
Teachers are not alone in wondering how to ensure that what they do is
helping to achieve their aims. Monitoring the relation between pupils'
experience and their schools' aims is the last topic we tackle in this chapter.

In their most public form a school's aims are likely to be broad and
general, like the six points we suggested on p. 15. Such statements are
appropriate as a basis for telling parents and governors about the school.
But they are only the first step in helping teachers to decide what to teach.
More specific aims are needed for each group of pupils. And as we said
on p. 23, in specifying the type and level of skill they intend their pupils
to acquire teachers come near to setting themselves precise aims. This is
equally worthwhile, but much more difficult in the parts of the curriculum
concerned with values and attitudes.

There might therefore be several different levels of aims in a school. A
primary school might perhaps have three or four: a general statement for
the whole school, a more detailed statement relating to each of the points
in the overall statement, another more detailed statement for each area of
the curriculum, and a very detailed statement for each year or class.

If one of the school's general aims were in part to foster an appreciation
of human achievements in art and music, its more detailed statements
might include teaching every child to read tonic sol fa and to sing in unison,
four out of five children to play a wind instrument and three out of five
to play a second wind or a string instrument. To achieve these aims would

Table 4

PRACTICAL SKILLS	Staff	Stamp
1 Has used simple tools safely.		
2 Can select appropriate tools.		
3 Has used powered tools safely.		
4 Can understand simple scientific terms.		
5 Can make and record accurate measurements or observations.		
6 Is competent in the use of electricity in workshop or home.		
7 Is competent in basic cookery.		
8 Can use a sewing machine.		
9 Can interpret simple graphs and statistics.		
10 Can choose and follow a route on a map.		

PERSONAL AND SOCIAL SKILLS	Staff	Stamp
1 Can work well as a member of a group.		
2 Takes pride in his/her appearance.		
3 Has a good attendance record.		
4 Is normally punctual.		
5 Enjoys playing games and sport.		
6 Can swim 25 m.		
7 Can work well without supervision.		
8 Can organize his/her work efficiently.		
9 Understands and can apply simple first aid.		
10 Has attended a school residential course/ expedition.		

PRACTICAL SKILLS

	Staff	Stamp
11 Can work accurately from a drawing or pattern.		
12 Can type accurately at 30 w.p.m.		
13 Can play a musical instrument.		
14 Can express ideas in sketch or diagram form.		
15 Shows good artistic skill.		

PERSONAL AND SOCIAL SKILLS

	Staff	Stamp
11 Has satisfactorily followed a child-care course.		
12 Has held a position of responsibility at school.		
13 Can receive and escort school visitors.		
14 Shows a capacity for organization and leadership.		
15 Can address an audience in public.		

clearly need decisions about what music children of 7 and 8 were to learn, and what levels of competence they should acquire.

One school had identified sixty skills and competencies which fifth-year pupils are expected to acquire.[11] Fifteen of the skills are mathematical, fifteen to do with communication, fifteen practical and fifteen personal and social. The last two groups are listed above.

A record of this kind serves several purposes. Used as it is with fifth-year pupils it is also intended to be of value to prospective employers, but it has an even more immediate value in providing targets and motivation for the pupils. For teachers and school it provides a way of checking whether what is taught and learned is properly related to these detailed aims, and to the school's overall aims.

Checkpoints for action

1. How can a school most usefully make a start on finding out what

each child's experience is and what the children learn from these experiences?

2. What means of monitoring content does the school intend to use?
3. Does the school have means of knowing how time is allocated and whether it is spent effectively?
4. Has the school adopted satisfactory ways of monitoring continuity and progression in its own curriculum, and in its links with other schools?
5. What steps has the school taken to develop progression in its pupils' curriculum?
6. Is the school able to show a direct link between the classroom experiences it provides and its overall aims?

IV. Assessment

The previous chapter was about monitoring the curriculum, or finding out what is happening. This chapter is about assessment, or judging the effectiveness of what is being done.

Many kinds of judgement are made about schools and their pupils. But we are writing still for practising teachers in the context of these papers about the curriculum. Our concern is therefore with how these teachers can set about assessing a school's procedures for deciding, planning and monitoring the curriculum. Teachers are more used to assessing the performance, progress and potential of individual pupils. They use these assessments to inform parents and to inform prospective employers or colleges of further and higher education. But the information they gather for these reports could also help in assessing the school's performance, reporting to governors and the local authority, and reviewing the school's terms of reference, aims and methods.

Terms of reference

They might start from some of the points we made in Chapter I, 'A rationale for the curriculum'. We discussed several ways of looking at the curriculum through the underlying principles and aims on which it rests, the kinds of experience and forms of knowledge it opens up, the modes of teaching and learning it uses, and the values, attitudes, skills and capacity for self-expression it seeks to develop.

We suggested that the curriculum should reflect the diversity of human nature and the capacity schools have to contribute to personal and social growth. Teachers might usefully ask whether their curriculum does this better now than it used to do, as well as the curriculum in any other school they know, or as well as it might. Is the range of experience, knowledge and modes of teaching and learning as wide as it should be? Could pupils learn more from the existing range? Could teachers do any more or should they do anything differently to develop desired values, attitudes and behaviour? The answers to questions like these provide a basis for assessment, review, and further development.

Similar questions about how a school plans and monitors its curriculum might provide a basis for systematic assessment of these procedures too.

What each child takes away: the effective curriculum

The most important test is whether these procedures enable pupils to learn what their teachers intend. We suggested on p. 15 that schools have the capacity to help their pupils in at least six ways. Schools which made these their own aims could assess their success if they were able to measure the knowledge, understanding and personal qualities their pupils take away. But much of the evidence unfolds slowly over many years, and even then it is more easily felt than measured. The school's specific contribution is not easily disentangled from other influences. And secondary schools cannot usually hope to keep in touch with enough of their former pupils to know how a whole cohort measure up to adult and working life. Though primary schools might gain by knowing more about the strengths and weaknesses their pupils demonstrate at secondary school, there seems to be no practicable way in which teachers can assess their success in achieving their overall aims.

Achieving specific aims

They must therefore look for other evidence. Success in achieving the specific aims we recommend for each year and class is one possible kind of evidence. If properly thought out these specific aims will be consistent with the overall aims; they are indeed no more than stages in a child's progression to maturity. Success in achieving a school's specific or intermediate aims is therefore a legitimate basis for assessment.

Sometimes the level of achievement is easily measured and easily quantified. It might even be appropriate sometimes to express an assessment in numerical terms: a school is doing well, we might say, if 80 per cent of its pupils achieve a certain standard in some specified skill.

Evidence of this kind is not often to be had. Teachers are more likely to have to rely on their own judgement, subjective indeed but trained, experienced and systematic.

Matching standards and ability

This professional expertise is needed in planning, monitoring and assessment to ensure that children are given work which matches their development and to judge whether the standard of their work matches their ability. The idea of matching standards and ability was accepted in the Schools Council's Science 5–13 Project, and in Her Majesty's Inspectors' primary survey:

> The relationship between the standard of work children in the groups were doing and that which they were considered by HMI to be capable of doing in each subject is referred to, for reasons of simplicity, as 'match' . . . A reasonably satisfactory match was recorded when the tasks presented to children were related to their existing skills and knowledge, when there was evidence of progression in the work and when there was evidence of acquisition of further skill, information or understanding.[1]

Agreeing standards

The idea of matching work to children's capability is potentially useful. It demands first an intuitive feel for quality, the ability to recognize good work. Teachers might usefully explore how to develop this skill. More open discussion of the criteria used in judging a piece of work might be a helpful way of finding whether teachers usually agree about what constitutes a good match.

Teachers might also examine a range of their pupils' work to find out what it can tell them about the effect of their teaching. They might take several pieces of work from one age group, work in several subjects or work from pupils of different ages. Discussion of a selection of pupils' work would amount to an informal cross-moderation of their pupils' learning.

Active involvement in the external examination system has already enabled many teachers to acquire a great deal of experience in assessing and moderating standards of work. What we are suggesting is that schools should increasingly apply these skills in assessing their own effectiveness.

Observing and recording

Teachers may like to use some sort of checklist as an aide memoire in the process of self-assessment. The following list is recommended in *Learning through science* as an aid to making and recording observations on primary children's scientific development.[2]

Curiosity...............................					
Originality					
Willingness to co-operate..................					
Perseverance...........................					
Open-mindedness					
Self-criticism					
Responsibility					
Independence...........................					
Observing..............................					
Problem solving.........................					
Raising questions					
Exploring					
Finding patterns in observation					
Communicating verbally					
Communicating non-verbally					
Applying learning					
Cause and effect					
Classification					
Weight					
Length					
Area					
Volume................................					
Time					
Life-cycle					
....					
....					

These attributes are detailed on a five-point scale. Each attribute is defined to indicate the extremes and the means of the scale being used. For example:

CURIOSITY

Often seems unaware of new things and shows little sign of interest even when they are pointed out.

Is attracted by new things but looks at them only superficially or for a short time; asks questions mostly about what things are, where they come from rather than about how or why they work or relate to other things.

Shows interest in new or unusual things and notices details. Seeks by questioning or action to find out about and to explain causes and relationships.

Teachers may find it helpful to use a similar sort of framework to record their observations and appraisal of their pupils' language development.

Joan Tough has suggested a framework for fostering children's use of language;[3] teachers might wish to record characteristics such as the following:

  i How often do children use speech to draw attention to their own needs or to maintain their own status by defence or assertion?
 ii How often do they use language to extend or promote action and to secure collaboration? How often to accompany action, or to control and direct it?
iii How often to refer to past experience, or to contemplate the future – to instigate or predict?
 iv How often to reason, to recognize and offer solutions to problems, to contemplate alternatives in real or imagined contexts?
  v How often to project through the imagination, how often to project beyond the use of concrete materials to create an imagined situation – to project into the experiences and feelings of other people, to provide background 'scenery' for a play?
 vi How often to address themselves, how often to address other children or adults?

Notes on these points enable teachers to make a careful appraisal of each child's language development.

The next example shows how a similar checklist might be used to keep a record of learning skills.[4]

LEARNING SKILLS	Not yet	Yes	Does well
a. Skims skilfully for main idea.			
b. Can scan for specific detail.			
c. Is able to use several sources of information in project work.			
d. Can locate information in			
i different types of books – textbooks, atlas, yearbook, encyclopedia			
ii the library – card catalogues, index			
iii Maps, charts and graphs			
iv Can use:			
(a) table of contents			
(b) an index			
(c) a glossary			
(d) footnotes			
(e) an appendix.			
e. Can follow instructions.			
f. Is able to take effective notes.			
g. Is able to remember what is read and has a method of recall.			

In each of these examples a teacher would use the notes on each child to help that child. The notes on a whole class or a representative sample of pupils could be a useful means of assessing the curriculum and the teaching.

Assessing wider aims

Such checklists sometimes seem to bypass a school's most important general aims. Recognizing this, the authors of *Learning through science* recommend a set of questions designed to help teachers to make a more thorough assessment of their success in achieving these aims.

Do the pupils talk to each other about their work?

Do they initiate activities which are new to the classroom?

Do they persist over a period of days, weeks or months on things which capture their interest?

Do they have real interests of their own?

Are they able to say 'I don't know', with the expectation that they are going to do something about finding out?

Do they exhibit any initiative, have they developed any skill in finding out what they want to know?

Do they continue to wonder?

Can they deal with differences of opinion or differences in results on a reasonably objective basis without being completely swayed by considerations of social status?

Are they capable of intense involvement? Have they ever had a passionate commitment to anything?

Do they have a sense of humour which can find expression in relation to things which are important to them?

Do they continue to explore things which are not assigned outside school as well as within?

Can they afford to make mistakes freely and profit from them?

Do they reflect upon their errors and learn from them?

Do they challenge ideas and interpretations with the purpose of reaching deeper understandings?

Are they charitable and open in dealing with ideas with which they do not agree?

Can they listen to each other?

Are they willing to attempt to express ideas about which they have only a vague and intuitive awareness?

Are they able to make connections between things which seem superficially unrelated?

Are they flexible in problem solving?

Are they willing to argue with others?

Can they suspend judgement?

Are they capable of experiencing freshly and vividly?

Do they know how to get help when they need it and to refuse help when appropriate?

Are they self-propelling?

Can they accept guidance without having to have things prescribed?

Are they stubborn about holding on to views which are not popular?

Can they deal with distractions, avoid being at the mercy of the environment?

Are they intellectually responsible?

Do they recognise conflicting evidence or conflicting points of view?

Do they recognise their own potential in growing towards competence?[5]

The authors say 'probably the staff of any primary or middle school would be proud to pass on to the secondary school children possessing the potential these questions imply'. We believe any teachers, whatever the age of their pupils, whatever their specialism, could usefully adopt and adapt these questions.

The ways of recording children's scientific development, language development, learning skills and personal development described in this chapter are examples only. Similar observations and records might be made of other aspects of children's development.

Maintaining records like these is a formidable task. But their value is such that perhaps all teachers should ask whether they can do a thoroughly professional job without records of this kind. The process of recording detailed observations will itself develop a teacher's capacity to observe pupils precisely, and the records with help teachers to match their pupils' work to their stages of development and standards of work. Then when pupils move on to another school or leave school for employment the records of detailed observation can provide the material for detailed and helpful reports or profiles. Given the limitations of any other record of achievement, secondary schools ought perhaps to develop their capacity to write detailed profiles of all their pupils.

Above all, in the context of this chapter on assessing a school's curriculum, the profiles of a whole age group provide the best internal evidence of the school's performance.

There is other internal evidence of a school's performance. Teachers get immediate evidence of their own effectiveness from the questions their pupils ask and the answers they give to the teachers' own questions. Many teachers use quick tests to establish whether their pupils have mastered a topic, and the pupils' written work provides additional evidence. Teachers can also use internal school examinations as another way of checking the effectiveness of their teaching. The examination papers themselves, and the marked scripts, would provide even more valuable evidence of the relation between what teachers are testing and what they are rewarding, and the school's overall aims. Head and staff might usefully scrutinize a set of internal examination papers to see how well they and the marking scheme reflect the terms of reference agreed in the first stage of thinking about the curriculum. The degree of match between scripts, exam papers and terms of reference is a fair measure of a school's success in achieving what it set out to do.

A school's teachers have their own professional reasons for wishing to assess their school's effectiveness, and their skills equip them to carry out much of the assessment. They may also be able to help others outside the school who have their own reasons for assessing it, and learn at the same time from the somewhat different values and perspectives outsiders bring to bear. Schools have some obligation to report to parents, governors and local authority. The parents collectively and other members of the local community are well placed to assess some aspects of a school's performance, and it might be useful sometimes to find some way of gathering their views systematically.

The governing body, fortified by experience and sometimes by professional advice from the local authority or Her Majesty's Inspectorate, engages with staff in a regular process of discussion, assessment and review. The more governing body and staff share a common understanding of the school's purpose and success, the more likely the governing body is to be able to defend and help the school when necessary.

The same is also true of a school's relations with its local authority. In meeting their statutory duty to provide education, local authorities need to satisfy themselves that each of their schools is providing a satisfactory curriculum. Most employ advisers, inspectors and other officers qualified in education to help them do this. Sometimes local authorities undertake a formal school inspection, but more typically their officers' expertise is available to help schools agree terms of reference and find ways of planning, monitoring and assessing.

Schools may also find help in their local or regional colleges of education, polytechnics or universities. Departments with a specific responsibility for initial or in-service teacher training are the most obvious sources, but some of the staff in some departments of psychology, social science, management and others may offer their special expertise to help schools.

Another useful approach to assessment is to compare a school's terms of reference, its procedures and its curriculum with the views of Her Majesty's Inspectorate. Their reports on primary and secondary schools are incomparable surveys of primary and secondary education in the late 1970s. Their *View of the Curriculum* presents a series of stimulating suggestions with which teachers might test the assumptions on which a school's curriculum rests. Their education surveys and their series of matters for discussion provide a basis for critical assessment of particular aspects of the curriculum, as do the reports of the Assessment of Performance Unit on children's performance in mathematics and English.

Schools may find it helpful to use questions from an item bank or other standardized tests to see how the performance of their own pupils compares with the norm for the item or test. External examinations like the General Certificate of Education and the Certificate of Secondary Education provide another point of comparison between standards nationally and those of a single school. These external examinations are designed to place the candidates in order of merit, so their results are widely used in selecting entrants to employment or the next stage of education or training. This function is so important that schools often make success in external examinations one of their specific aims for the pupils of 14 to 18. But external examinations and tests are usually concerned with only a limited part of what a school is trying to achieve for its pupils. For that reason an examination certificate is of limited value even for pupils with successes in several subjects. The examination results need to be included in a full profile of a pupil's achievements.

Its pupils' success in external examinations is of course an important means of assessing a school. But given the close relation between examination success and such matters as social class, race, parental support and measured intelligence, the examination pass rate needs to be interpreted with care.

Comparing the results with their own informed view of their pupils' abilities would provide teachers with one means of assessment. Knowing their pupils and their background, and knowing the occasional eccentricities of examinations, teachers are well able to use their own pupils' results as a means of assessing what they have taught and how they have taught it.

Summary

In this chapter we have tried to show both how hard it is to assess a school's procedures for deciding, planning and monitoring its curriculum, and how some indicative evidence can be gathered. Success in achieving specific aims, providing various kinds of experience, introducing different forms of knowledge, using varied modes of teaching and learning, developing values, attitudes, skills and the capacity for self-expression are all legitimate approaches to assessment. Comparing a school's policy and practice with the published views of HMI on schools may be a useful basis for assessment. Comparing the school's policy and practice with private reports and comments on the school is another.

Pupils' attainments offer a different approach to assessment. The idea of a match between attainment and capability may be helpful, particularly in interpreting the results of external examinations, and developing a feeling for standards.

A teacher's professional expertise consists in large part of this ability to assess standards and judge capability. Both depend on careful observation, appraisal and recording of children's work and development. We hope our examples of how this might be done in science, language and learning skills will encourage teachers to develop similar checklists in other areas of the curriculum.

Other kinds of evidence might also be useful. We have not written anything about what a school does in public, its exhibitions, concerts, plays, journeys, games and community work. Teachers can use these too to fill out their own assessments. People outside a school may know it best through these public activities, and be inclined to give them greater significance than teachers do. To restore the balance teachers may need to find ways of presenting to parents, governors and local authorities the evidence on which they base their own assessments.

Assessment is part of the systematic process we mentioned in Chapter I, in which experience and thought reinforce each other. By clarifying aims, refining methods and assessing success, every school can hope to be a better school, whose pupils enjoy a broad, common and wholly effective curriculum.

Checkpoints for action

1. What has the school done to compare its achievements with the terms of reference it decided on?
2. What systems has the school adopted for assessing individual pupils and taking appropriate action to advise and guide them and their parents?
3. Can the records of pupil assessment be maintained and used easily?
4. What light do the pupils' achievements throw on the school's performance?

5. Has the school made use of its parent body, its local community, its governors and its local education authority as critical friends in helping in its self-assessment?

6. What use does the school make of external examination results, national work in assessment and national reports in assessing its own performance?

Conclusion

We described our aims in the introduction to this handbook. Now we have planned and published it we should welcome your help in monitoring its use and assessing its effectiveness.

Your comments on these working papers would be the best indication of whether they meet a need. Accounts of your own work on the curriculum would help us to produce a richer and better second edition.

We hope the handbook will be a useful basis for workshops and seminars on planning the curriculum. It might also be helpful in local evaluative or case studies. We would be delighted to know if it is used in these ways and particularly pleased to see any reports or papers which arise from these activities. We might perhaps be able to help to fund local groups which wanted to do something of this sort.

In planning this handbook we wondered whether it might be the first of a series. Some teachers have suggested that the Council could usefully prepare more detailed statements about objectives and skills, for different age groups and different subjects. It has also been suggested that we might try to identify exactly what knowledge and skills the study of traditional subjects develops.

Both these tasks seem appropriate for the Council. Before embarking on them we should find it helpful to know whether teachers would welcome more detailed papers of the kind suggested.

References

Chapter I. A rationale for the curriculum

1. Department of Education and Science, *Special Educational Needs*, Report of the Committee of Enquiry into the Education of Handicapped Children and Young People [The Warnock Report], HMSO, 1978, p. 5.
2. This list is based on the aims of the common core proposed by the Further Education Curriculum Review and Development Unit, *A Basis for Choice*, Report of a Study Group on Post-16 Pre-Employment Courses [The Mansell Report], FEU, June 1979, p. 42.
3. *Early experiences*, Macdonald Educational for the Schools Council, 1972, p. 17.
4. The Schools Council's Science 5–13 Project developed these ideas in *Using the environment 1: Early explorations*, Macdonald Educational, 1974.
5. Joan Tough, *Talking and Learning: a guide to fostering communication skills in nursery and infant schools*, Ward Lock Educational for the Schools Council, 1977, p. 240.
6. Department of Education and Science, *Primary education in England*, HMSO, 1978.
7. P. H. Hirst and R. S. Peters, *The Logic of Education*, Routledge & Kegan Paul, 1970, pp. 63–4.
8. D. Lawton, *Social Change, Educational Theory and Curriculum Planning*, University of London Press, 1973, p. 46.
9. Department of Education and Science, *Curriculum 11–16*, HMSO, 1977.

Chapter II. Planning the curriculum

1. J. Brierley, *Children's Well-Being: Growth, Development and Learning*

from Conception to Adolescence, NFER, Slough, 1980, p. 76.
2. ibid., p. 129.
3. Department of Education and Science, *Primary education in England*, HMSO, 1978, p. 37.
4. Department of Education and Science, *Aspects of secondary education in England*, HMSO, 1979, p. 42.
5. B. Wilcox and P. Eustace, *Tooling up for Curriculum Review*, NFER, Slough, 1980.
6. F. B. Salt, Headteacher, South Hunsley School, Humberside, in *Schools Council News* No. 33, Summer 1980, p. 4.
7. Derived from 'Personal and social development in the school curriculum', a background paper by Trevor Williams and Norman Williams in the Schools Council Health Education 13–18 Project's *Co-ordinator's Guide*, p. R41 (xiii–xiv). The project is based at the Health Education Unit of the University of Southampton.
8. E. Briault and F. Smith, *Falling Rolls in Secondary Schools*, NFER, Slough, 1980, Part One, p. 90.
9. Draft report from the OECD Sparsely Populated Areas Project, made available to the Schools Council and mentioned in Briault and Smith, op. cit., Part One, p. 87.
10. Irene Robertson, *Language across the curriculum: four case studies* (Schools Council Working Paper 67), Methuen Educational, 1980.
11. Department of Education and Science, *A framework for the school curriculum*, HMSO, 1980, p. 3.

Chapter III. Monitoring the curriculum

1. Welsh Office, *Literacy and numeracy and examination achievements in Wales*, Report of a conference held at Mold, March 1978, HMSO, 1978, p. 27.
2. Irene Robertson, *Language across the curriculum: four case studies* (Schools Council Working Paper 67), Methuen Educational, 1980, pp. 65–6, 77, 98, 103–11.
3. P. D. Neal, Headteacher, Perry Common School, Birmingham, personal communication.
4. 'Headmaster's Diary', *The Times Educational Supplement*, 15 August 1980.
5. Continuing Mathematics Project *Teacher's Handbook*, Longman for the Schools Council, 1976.
6. Department of Education and Science, *A framework for the school curriculum*, HMSO, 1980.

7. Penelope B. Weston, *Framework for the curriculum: a study in secondary schooling*, NFER, Slough, 1977, p. 162.
8. Unpublished materials generated in individual schools by teachers working with SMILE.
9. Report of the Schools Council Continuity and Development Project, in preparation.
10. P. D. Neal, Headteacher, Perry Common School, Birmingham, personal communication.
11. Evesham High School, Hereford and Worcester, internal document.

Chapter IV. Assessment

1. Department of Education and Science, *Primary education in England*, HMSO, 1978, p. 80.
2. *Learning through science: Formulating a School Policy*, Macdonald Educational for the Schools Council, 1980, p. 27.
3. Joan Tough, *Talking and Learning: a guide to fostering communication skills in nursery and infant schools*, Ward Lock Educational for the Schools Council, 1977, p. 23.
4. Unpublished material used in early discussions on a recording system in Rochdale Local Education Authority.
5. *Learning through science*, op. cit., pp. 27–8.

Reading list

This list includes some books mentioned in the text and a small selection of others which readers may find helpful.

D. Barnes. *From Communication to Curriculum.* Penguin, 1976.

J. Brierley. *Children's Well-Being.* NFER, Slough, 1980.

J. S. Bruner. *Toward a Theory of Instruction.* Harvard University Press, Boston, Mass., 1966.

Department of Education and Science. *Education in Schools*, a consultative document [The Green Paper]. HMSO, 1977.

Curriculum 11–16 [The Red Book]. HMSO, 1977.

Special Educational Needs [The Warnock Report]. HMSO, 1978.

Primary education in England, a survey by HM Inspectors of Schools. HMSO, 1978.

Aspects of secondary education in England, a survey by HM Inspectors of Schools. HMSO, 1979.

A View of the Curriculum [HMI Matters for Discussion Series]. HMSO, 1979.

A framework for the school curriculum. HMSO, 1980.

Exeter University School of Education. *The Core Curriculum: Perspectives 2.* University of Exeter, 1980.

P. H. Hirst. *Knowledge and the Curriculum.* Routledge & Kegan Paul, 1975.

M. Holt. *The Common Curriculum.* Routledge & Kegan Paul, 1978.

R. Hooper. *The Curriculum: Context, Design and Development.* Oliver & Boyd, Edinburgh, 1971.

R. M. Jones. *Fantasy and Feeling in Education.* Penguin, 1972.

D. Lawton. *Class, Culture and the Curriculum.* Routledge & Kegan Paul, 1975.

The Politics of the School Curriculum. Routledge & Kegan Paul, 1980.

D. Lawton *et al. Theory and Practice of Curriculum Studies.* Routledge & Kegan Paul, 1978.

H. G. MacIntosh. *Assessing Attainment in the Classroom.* Hodder & Stoughton, 1976.

R. M. Pirsig. *Zen and the Art of Motorcycle Maintenance.* Bodley Head, 1974.

W. A. Reid. *Thinking about the curriculum.* Routledge & Kegan Paul, 1978.

M. Rutter *et al. Fifteen Thousand Hours: secondary schools and their effects on children.* Open Books, 1979.

Scottish Council for Research in Education. *Pupils in Profile*. Hodder & Stoughton, 1977.

L. A. Stenhouse. *An Introduction to Curriculum Research and Development*. Heinemann Educational, 1975.

L. A. Stenhouse (ed.). *Curriculum Research and Development in Action*. Heinemann Educational, 1980.

J. P. White. *Towards a Compulsory Curriculum*. Routledge & Kegan Paul, 1973.

B. Wilcox and P. Eustace. *Tooling up for Curriculum Review*. NFER, Slough, 1980.

R. W. Witkin. *The Intelligence of Feeling*. Heinemann Educational, 1974.

Members of the Working Group

J. R. G. Tomlinson (*Chairman*) — Director of Education, Cheshire, and Chairman, Schools Council

D. W. Armstrong — Deerness Valley Comprehensive School, Ushaw Moor, Durham

J. Chambers — Regents Park Secondary School, Shirley, Southampton

L. Cooper — Deputy Headmaster, Sherburn High School, Leeds

J. C. Davenport — Woodhouse Park Infant School, Wythenshawe, Manchester

V. M. Glauert — Headmistress, Blyth-Jex School, Norwich

P. L. Griffin — Windsor Clive County Junior School, Ely

R. Hemington (*until September 1980*) — Dinas Bran School, Llangollen, Clwyd

M. J. Henley — County Education Officer, Northamptonshire

SI D. Hollingsworth — HM Inspectorate of Schools

Professor D. Lawton — Institute of Education, University of London

D. I. Morgan — W. R. Tuson College, Preston, Lancashire

A. Noonan — Headmaster, Holyrood RC Junior Mixed School, Watford

M. D. Phipps (*until May 1980*) — Department of Education and Science

P. W. Syme (*from July 1980*) — Department of Education and Science

SI A. F. Turberfield — HM Inspectorate of Schools

I. Williams — Headmaster, Pennard Primary School, Gower, Swansea

J. Yeomans — National Confederation of Parent-Teacher Associations

Schools Council staff

J. Mann — Secretary

K. McWilliams — Deputy Secretary

R. C. Abbott — Director, Programme 1, Purpose and Planning in Schools

M. Plaskow — Curriculum Officer

D. G. Smetherham — Educational Researcher